Everything You Need to Know About

Cerebral Palsy

People with cerebral palsy benefit from the love and support of their families.

Everything You Need to Know About
Cerebral Palsy

Dion Pincus

Rosen Publishing Group, Inc./New York

For Kyo Navarre and Amber Dee:
my big little, and my little big

Published in 2000 by The Rosen Publishing Group, Inc.
29 East 21st Street, New York, NY 10010

Copyright © 2000 by The Rosen Publishing Group, Inc.

First Edition

Library of Congress Cataloging-in-Publication Data

Pincus, Dion.
    Everything you need to know about cerebral palsy / Dion Pincus.
      p.   cm — (The need to know library)
    Includes bibliographical references and index.
    Summary: Describes the causes and consequences of cerebral palsy, the most common lifelong disability in America, as well as offering coping strategies and resources for teens with cerebral palsy.
    ISBN 0-8239-2960-4
    1. Cerebral Palsy Juvenile literature. 2. Cerebral palsied Juvenile literature. 3. Cerebral palsied children Juvenile literature. [1. Cerebral palosy.] I. Title II. Series.
RC388.P565 1999
616.8'3dc21
                                                                    CIP
                                                                    AC

Manufactured in the United States of America

Contents

Introduction

Kenneth, now age twelve, remembers what it was like for him to grow up as a child with cerebral palsy:

When I was about a year old, my mom first realized that something was wrong with me. I couldn't sit up straight, I couldn't stand, I was still crawling on the floor and pulling myself along with my hands. When my mother finally spoke to my pediatrician about it, he referred her to another doctor. The other doctor couldn't see me for like six months because he had so many other appointments. But when we did get to see him, he told my parents that he thought I had cerebral palsy. He said he couldn't be sure, and he suggested that my mom go to United Cerebral Palsy, which is an organization that specializes in the care of kids with cerebral palsy. The doctors there did a lot of tests on me—they measured some of my movements and watched me a lot—and they agreed. I did have CP. By then I was two.

I was classified as a spastic quadriplegic, which means I had some spasticity in my arms and legs. Spasticity is like stiffness, so when I moved my arms and legs they jerked instead of moving in a smooth way. And when I tried to walk, my legs would cross so I could take only about four steps before losing my balance and falling down.

I got into the Cerebral Palsy Program. The main purpose of this program was to make me independent. The people at the program taught me important skills, like how to get into and out of my clothing. They even toilet trained me, which wasn't so easy. Imagine how difficult it was for me to learn how to use the toilet when I was having trouble just keeping my balance while standing up! I was in the program for only a few hours a day at first, and as I got older it was like a regular school from nine to three. I stayed in the program until I was about six years old.

Besides helping me, the people at the Cerebral Palsy Program really helped my parents. There's a branch near where we live and my mom and dad got very involved with the parents' support group. One of the problems that parents of kids with disabilities have is finding baby-sitters to take care of their kids so they can go out once in a while, like for dinner or a movie. The parents in the support group all took turns baby-sitting for each other. Since all the kids had CP, all the parents knew exactly what to do.

I'm in the sixth grade now, and I do pretty well in school. I have some great friends, and all my teachers have gotten to know me over the years. And absolutely, my favorite subject is science. I think that when I get older and go to college, I'd like to study all about the human body and become a research scientist. I want to work to help people just like me.

A Definition of Cerebral Palsy

Cerebral palsy, or CP, is an overall name given to describe a variety of specific symptoms. The words "cerebral palsy" are used to describe a medical condition that affects control of the muscles. "Cerebral" means anything in the head or brain, and "palsy" refers to anything wrong with control of the muscles or joints in the body. When we say that individuals have cerebral palsy, it means that because of injuries to their brains (that's the cerebral part), they are not able to use some of the muscles in their bodies in the normal way (that's the palsy part). People who have cerebral palsy may not be able to walk, talk, eat, or play in the same way as others.

It is important to know that cerebral palsy is not an illness or a disease. You can't catch it from someone else, and it doesn't get worse over time. However, cerebral palsy is not something you "grow out of." Children who have cerebral palsy will have it all their lives.

What This Book Does

Whether you are a person with cerebral palsy or know someone who is, this book is intended to help you gather as much basic information as you can about the realities of the condition and the people who live with them. As we go through the chapters, we'll discuss the facts concerning cerebral palsy and some of the myths surrounding it. You'll learn what the different forms of cerebral palsy are, some of the causes for the disorder, and how cerebral palsy is treated. But more important, perhaps, is the picture you'll get of what Kenneth and other kids and teens like him have in common—they have been through a lot, they have refused to feel sorry for themselves, and they have not allowed their disability to impair their potential.

Children with CP tend to have trouble grasping objects, crawling, and walking.

Chapter One

Cerebral Palsy: Then and Now

Then: A History

To find the first medical descriptions of cerebral palsy, we have to go back to the 1860s, when an English surgeon named William Little wrote about a puzzling disorder he had noticed in some children. It seemed that in the first years of their lives, this disorder caused stiff, tightening muscles mostly in the children's legs and sometimes in their arms. These children had trouble grasping objects, crawling, and walking. They did not get better as they grew up, but they didn't seem to get any worse, either. Their condition, which was called Little's disease for many years, is now known as spastic diplegia.

People with spastic diplegia have very tight and stiff muscles (that's the "spastic" part) in either both of their legs or both of their arms (that's the "di" part). These stiff muscles make it hard for a person to move correctly (that's the "plegia" part, which is a Latin word for paralyzed or weak). Spastic diplegia is just one of several disorders that affect the muscles that control our movement and are grouped together under the term "cerebral palsy."

William Little felt that the reason many of these children were born with this condition was because there were difficulties during their births. He wrote that their condition seemed to be caused by a lack of oxygen during birth and that this lack of oxygen had somehow damaged the brain tissues that control movement.

Other doctors, however, felt that the disorder might have its beginnings not during or after birth, but earlier in life, while the brain was still developing in the womb. But it was William Little's theory—that cerebral palsy was caused by birth complications—that was the most acceptable to physicians, families, and even medical researchers. Until very recently.

Now: Some New Discoveries

In the 1980s, a government study was conducted of more than 35,000 births, and the surprising result was that complications during birth accounted for only a very small number of cases of cerebral palsy—less than 10 percent. The overwhelming conclusion of the study was this: In most cases of cerebral palsy, no one single cause could be found.

The government study in the 1980s led doctors to re-explore their medical theories and the way research about cerebral palsy is done. Since then, there have been important changes in the way we understand cerebral palsy and the people who are affected by it.

Today, for example, doctors are able to identify infants with cerebral palsy very early in life, which gives youngsters the best opportunity for developing to their full potential. And new research has led to better ways of finding and treating problems that may actually cause cerebral palsy. Because of this new research, certain conditions that have been known to cause cerebral palsy, such as rubella (German measles) and jaundice, can now be prevented and treated.

Also, children today who have cerebral palsy are better able to be independent, to achieve, and to succeed in life by using specific physical, behavioral, and other therapies. And medications, braces, and even surgery can often improve muscle and nerve coordination, help treat other medical problems associated with cerebral palsy, and even prevent or correct deformities.

Just What Exactly Is Cerebral Palsy?

As we have said, cerebral palsy, also called CP, is an overall term used to describe a group of disorders that affect a person's ability to control the body's movements. The disorders appear in the first few years of a person's life and generally do not get worse over time.

13

SOME FACTS ABOUT CEREBRAL PALSY

Cerebral palsy is the most common lifelong physical disability in America.

The United Cerebral Palsy Association estimates that anywhere between 500,000 and 700,000 American children and adults currently have cerebral palsy. One in every 1,000 babies in the United States is diagnosed as having cerebral palsy.

Annually, it is estimated that 3,500 to 4,000 infants are born with this condition, and an additional 1,500 preschool age children acquire cerebral palsy as the result of accidents or abuse.

Cerebral palsy is not progressive (it doesn't get worse as you get older), it is not communicable (you can't "catch" it from someone else), it is not inherited (it is not a trait that is passed down from parents to children), and it is not a primary cause of death (people don't die from it).

The term "cerebral" refers to the brain's two halves, or hemispheres, and "palsy" describes any disorder that impairs control of body movement.

But let's not make a mistake here. It's not the muscles or nerves themselves that have something wrong with them. Actually, a person with cerebral palsy has perfectly fine muscles and nerves in his or her body. Instead, what is happening is that there is a problem with the development of, or damage to, those parts of the brain that control movement and posture. Those parts of the brain are called the motor areas. In short, what happens is that the muscles in the body are receiving the wrong instructions about what to do from the damaged part of the brain.

Causes of Cerebral Palsy

When we speak of cerebral palsy, we should know that it is not one disease with a single cause. In fact, it is not a disease at all. It is actually a group of disorders that are related, but which probably have different causes.

When a person acquires the disorder or disorders after birth, we say that the person has "acquired cerebral palsy." However, when the disorder or disorders are present at birth, we say that the person has "congenital cerebral palsy."

Acquired cerebral palsy
About 10 to 20 percent of children and adults who have cerebral palsy acquire the disorder after birth.

Acquired cerebral palsy generally results from brain damage in the first few months or years of life and often follows severe brain infections, such as viral encephalitis. Acquired cerebral palsy can also result from a head injury, most often from a motor vehicle accident, a fall, or child abuse.

Congenital cerebral palsy

People with congenital cerebral palsy are born with it, although it may not be detected for several months. In most cases, the cause of congenital cerebral palsy is unknown. However, thanks to recent research, scientists have been able to identify some factors during pregnancy or around the time of birth that can damage the important motor areas in the developing brain which control the way muscles in the body move. Some of these factors that may cause congenital cerebral palsy include:

+ Infections during pregnancy. German measles, or rubella, is caused by a virus that can infect pregnant women. This can be passed on by the mother to the unborn child, or fetus, still developing inside her, causing damage to the fetus's nervous system.

+ Jaundice in the infant. Bile pigments, which are normally found in small amounts in the bloodstream, are produced in the body when blood cells are destroyed. But when too many blood cells are destroyed too quickly, the yellow-colored bile pigments can build up and cause a condition called jaundice. If left untreated, severe jaundice can damage brain cells.

◆ Rh incompatibility. This is a blood condition where the mother's body produces immune cells, called antibodies, that destroy the fetus's blood cells. This often leads to a form of jaundice in the newborn.

◆ Severe oxygen shortage in the brain. A lack of oxygen caused by problems in breathing or a poor oxygen supply sometimes happens to babies during childbirth. If the supply of oxygen to the infant's brain is lowered for too long a time, the child may develop brain damage.

◆ Trauma or injury caused by a difficult labor and delivery. When a pregnant woman has difficulties giving birth, an obstetrician (a doctor who delivers newborns) may assist by using forceps—an instrument that grabs the baby by the head—to help pull the baby out. Improper use of the forceps may cause injury to the newborn's head or brain. Additionally, a breech delivery (where the baby's buttocks or legs come out first,

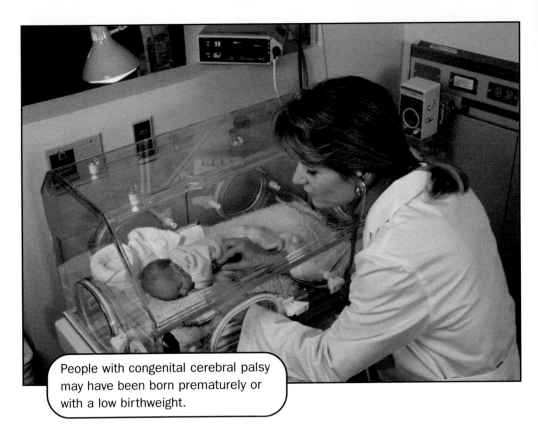

People with congenital cerebral palsy may have been born prematurely or with a low birthweight.

instead of the head) may cause an infant to have a lack of oxygen, which in turn can increase the possibility of brain damage.

◆ Low birthweight. Premature and low-birthweight babies (those born before the end of 37 weeks or with a birthweight of 5.5 pounds or less) have a higher risk for breathing complications, oxygen shortage, and brain damage than do full-term, normal-weight babies.

◆ Stroke. A stroke happens when there is bleeding in the brain. Bleeding in the brain has several causes, including broken or clogged blood vessels in the brain, or abnormal blood cells. A stroke in a fetus during pregnancy, or

MYTH:

Cerebral palsy always causes a profound handicap.

FACT:

A person with mild cerebral palsy may have a disability that is almost unnoticeable and require no special assistance at all.

in the newborn around the time of birth, can damage brain tissue.

Symptoms of Cerebral Palsy

Cerebral palsy has many different symptoms. Some are more, and some are less severe. An individual with cerebral palsy may have trouble with activities like writing, drawing, or cutting with scissors; experience trouble with maintaining his or her balance and walking; or be affected by uncontrollable movements and behaviors, such as twisting and turning motions of the hands, or drooling. And not only do different people have different symptoms, but those symptoms may even change over time in the individual.

Some people with cerebral palsy are also affected by other medical disorders, including epilepsy and seizures, blindness, deafness, or mental impairment.

The Four Different Forms of Cerebral Palsy

As we said earlier, a person with cerebral palsy has damage to the area of the brain that is in charge of muscle control. Depending on where the brain injury is, and how large it is, the person's muscle tone may be too tight, too loose, or a combination of both. Muscle tone is what lets us keep our bodies in a certain position, like sitting with our heads up to watch a movie in a theater. Changes in muscle tone are what allow us to move.

Spastic diplegia, the disorder first described by William Little, is only one of several disorders called cerebral palsy. Today, doctors classify cerebral palsy into four categories: spastic, athetoid, ataxic, and mixed.

Spastic cerebral palsy

If muscle tone is too high or too tight, the term "spastic"—stiffness or tightness of the muscles—is used to describe the type of cerebral palsy. Spastic cerebral palsy is the most common type of CP—about 70 to 80 percent of people with CP have this particular form. With spastic cerebral palsy, the muscles of the body are stiffly and permanently contracted. When a person without cerebral palsy performs a movement, some groups of muscles become tighter and some relax. When people with spastic cerebral palsy perform a movement, both groups of muscles may become tighter. These people may have difficulty moving from one position to another or letting go of something in their hands.

Doctors will often describe which type of spastic cerebral palsy a person has based on which limbs are affected. For example:

- Spastic diplegia affects either both arms or both legs. "Di" means two. In cases of diplegia, it's more common to have only the lower two limbs (legs) affected.

- Spastic hemiplegia, affects only one side of the body. "Hemi" means half. In hemiplegia, just the right arm and leg, or just the left arm and leg, are affected.

- Spastic quadriplegia affects all limbs on both sides of the body. "Quad" means four. With quadriplegia, there is difficulty with moving all parts of the body—face and trunk, as well as arms and legs.

- Spastic monoplegia is a rare condition that affects only one limb. "Mono" means one.

- Spastic triplegia which affects three limbs, is also fairly rare. "Tri" means three.

21

Athetoid cerebral palsy

If muscle tone is mixed—sometimes too high and sometimes too low—the term "athetoid" is used. Athetoid cerebral palsy affects about 10 to 20 percent of people who have CP. This form of cerebral palsy is characterized by uncontrolled, slow, or twisting movements of the body. Children and adults with athetoid cerebral palsy may have trouble holding themselves in an upright, steady position for sitting and walking, and often perform lots of involuntary movements. These movements are usually big and can affect the hands, feet, arms, or legs. In some cases, they also affect the muscles of the face and tongue, causing odd facial expressions, frowning, or drooling.

Ataxic cerebral palsy

If muscle tone is too low or too loose, the term "ataxic" is used. Affecting only 5 to 10 percent of persons with cerebral palsy, this form is the least common. Ataxia is the word used for unsteady, shaky movements, or tremors. Those with ataxic cerebral palsy often have poor coordination and balance, place their feet unusually far apart and walk unsteadily, and have trouble making quick or precise movements, such as writing, turning a page in a book, or buttoning a shirt.

Mixed

When muscle tone is too high in some specific muscles and too low in other specific muscles, the type of cerebral palsy is called mixed. It is quite common for persons with cerebral palsy to have symptoms of more than one of the previous three forms. The most common mixed form includes spasticity and athetoid movements, but other combinations are also possible.

No One Is to Blame

Almost all families of people with cerebral palsy worry about the cause and wonder why it happened. This is a very normal and understandable response. Parents often blame themselves for something they may or may not have done during the pregnancy or at birth. However, usually the event that caused the condition could not possibly have been prevented by them. It is far better if these families discuss their problems and share their concerns with each other, and with the professionals and other persons involved in the care of their children, than if they live in a state of continual guilt, blame, and worry.

Chapter Two

What's Going On with Me?

The Early Signs

Early signs of cerebral palsy usually appear before three years of age, and usually the parents are the first to suspect that their infant is not developing motor, language, or social skills normally. Infants with cerebral palsy are often slow to reach developmental milestones—skills and behaviors that are considered normal to have at certain ages—such as learning to roll over, sit, crawl, smile, or walk. When a child is slow to reach these developmental milestones, this is sometimes called developmental delay.

Some examples of developmental delay in normal skills and behaviors might be a child who cannot grasp a rattle by the age of three months, walk up steps by the age of eighteen months, or recognize three different colors by the age of thirty-six months. But remember that

24

the term "normal" is not set in stone. A child may gain individual skills earlier or later than other children.

Although children often acquire specific skills and behaviors at their own individual pace, significant delays in any or a combination of these skills and behaviors can raise red flags, or concerns. As a parent, a family member, or just someone who knows a child, it is important to educate yourself about delays in a child's development and any difficulties he or she might be having with various skills so that you can ask the right questions about your concerns.

What Happens Next?

A developmental delay in a child may actually be the first "red flag," or sign, of cerebral palsy to a parent or physician. Doctors can then test for CP in a number of ways. These include:

Testing for reflexes
Doctors look at several reflexes when testing for cerebral palsy, including one called the Moro reflex—a motion that looks like a hug—which babies make when they are held on their backs and tilted upward. Babies usually lose this reflex after six months, but babies with CP may continue to have it for a long time.

Looking for hand preference
During the first twelve months of life, babies do not usually show a tendency to use either the right or left

hand more often. But infants with spastic hemiplegia, for example, may develop a preference much earlier because the hand on the unaffected side of the body is stronger and more useful.

Ruling out other disorders

Since cerebral palsy is not progressive—meaning the condition does not get worse over time—doctors must explore whether movement problems might be caused by something else. So if a child is continuously losing motor skills, the problem is most likely something other than CP.

Ordering specialized tests

Doctors can order specialized tests both to diagnose cerebral palsy and to learn more about the possible cause. These tests include computerized tomography (CT), which creates a picture of the inside of the brain using X rays and a computer; magnetic resonance imaging (MRI), which creates an image of the brain using magnetic fields and radio waves; and ultrasonography, which creates a picture of the brain using sound waves.

Looking for other conditions that are linked to cerebral palsy

Doctors also diagnose cerebral palsy by looking for other associated conditions, such as seizure disorders, mental impairment, and vision or hearing problems.

- Seizure disorders are tested for by means of an electroencephalogram, or EEG, which

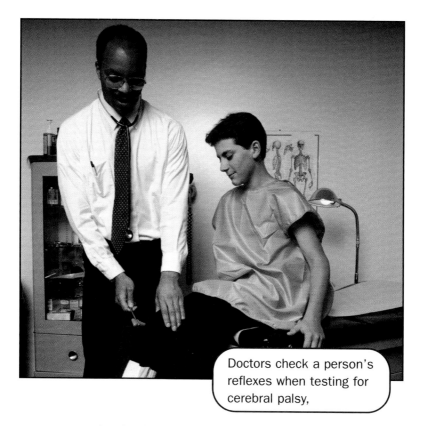

Doctors check a person's reflexes when testing for cerebral palsy,

records the brain's electrical currents and activity.

- A mental impairment is often checked for by means of intelligence tests.

- If problems with vision are suspected, a doctor may refer the person to an ophthalmologist (eye doctor). If a hearing impairment is suspected, a doctor may refer the person to an otologist (ear doctor).

Identifying conditions that are linked to cerebral palsy is important in helping a doctor make an accurate diagnosis of CP. And once these linked conditions have been identified, many of them can then be appropriately handled with specific treatments.

Associated Medical Disorders

Although it is true that many people who have cerebral palsy have no associated medical disorders at all, sometimes disorders that involve the brain do indeed cause other problems. Some of the more common medical disorders and problems associated with cerebral palsy include:

Drooling

Poor control of the muscles of the throat, mouth, and tongue can sometimes lead to drooling. Drooling can cause severe skin irritations and, because it is considered "socially unacceptable," can cause a person with this problem to feel even more isolated from other kids and friends because of embarrassment and shame. Although numerous treatments for drooling have been tested over the years, there is no one treatment that always helps.

Kids used to tease me all the time, says Li Fong, who is sixteen. They used to call me baby and stupid and other hurtful names because I had a problem with drooling. But what was I supposed to do? I couldn't control it. Every time I'd try to say more than ten words at a time, it was like my mouth was full of water and the words would drown. I was petrified! I was completely afraid to speak to people or to try to make friends.

I've been working with an occupational therapist, and she has been helping me to find ways to control my drooling—mostly by making me very aware of my body every time I do it, and by getting me to look at the patterns of when it seems to happen most. I've actually made some improvement, and I am slowly getting better at feeling like I can talk to people.

Seizures and epilepsy

A seizure happens when the brain—which is constantly sending out electrical messages to your body, such as to breathe or to move—sends out unusual electrical messages, very close together, that interrupt what you are doing. People who have seizures may stare, stop moving, lose control of their bodies, twitch, or fall down. When seizures happen over and over, the condition is called epilepsy.

Growth problems

Children with moderate to severe cerebral palsy may have a condition called "failure to thrive," where they seem to fall behind in their growth and development. In babies, this falling behind usually takes the form of too little weight-gain; in young children, it can appear as shortness; in teenagers, it may appear as a mixture of shortness and lack of sexual development.

Impaired vision or hearing

People with cerebral palsy may have a condition called strabismus—where the eyes do not line up and focus properly because of differences between the left and right eye muscles. People with CP may also have poor vision or blindness because of damage to the normal field of vision in only one eye, which happens to those whose CP affects only one side of the body. Impaired hearing is also more frequent among those with CP than those without.

Difficulty with talking

The speech problem that most people with CP have is called dysarthria. That means it is hard for them to control and coordinate the muscles needed to talk. Their speech may sound very slow and slurred, and their faces may look strained when they are trying to talk.

Mental impairment

Another disorder associated with cerebral palsy is mental impairment. A mental impairment may be of two different types. It may take the form of a learning disability, where there is a difficulty in processing certain kinds of information in a person of normal to above-normal intelligence; or it may take the form of mental retardation, where a person functions at lower-than-normal intelligence.

Cerebral palsy is a disability—it is not, however, who you are—and it is not something to be ashamed or fearful of.

Chapter Three

Living with Cerebral Palsy

There is no cure for cerebral palsy. But it most certainly can be treated. And treatment can often improve the quality of a person's life. The progress that has been made over the years in medical research helps many people with CP to enjoy full and wonderful lives.

There is no one therapy that works for all individuals with CP. Instead, a physician must work with a team of health care professionals first to identify a person's unique needs and impairments, and then to create an individual treatment plan that addresses them.

What Do You Mean, a "Treatment Plan"?

Some approaches that can be included in a treatment plan for someone with CP are drugs to control seizures; special braces to deal with muscle problems;

surgery; mechanical aids to help overcome impairments; counseling for emotional and psychological needs; and physical, occupational, speech, and behavioral therapies. Usually, the earlier treatment begins, the better chance a child has of overcoming his or her disability and learning new ways to accomplish difficult tasks.

The members of the treatment team for a child with cerebral palsy are professionals with a wide range of specialties. A typical treatment team might include:

- A physician, such as a pediatrician (children's doctor) or a pediatric neurologist (someone who specializes in the brain and nervous system of children). This physician is often the leader of the treatment team and works to pull together all the professional advice of the treatment team members into one plan.

- An orthopedist (someone who specializes in treating the bones, muscles, tendons, and other parts of the body's skeletal system). An orthopedist might be called on to treat muscle problems associated with cerebral palsy.

- A physical therapist, who creates special exercise programs to improve movement and strength in the large muscles of the body (arms, legs, torso).

A physical therapist will create special exercise programs to improve movement and strength in the large muscles of the body.

- An occupational therapist, who helps individuals improve the development of their small muscle movement (face, hands, feet, fingers, toes) and learn practical skills for daily living, school, and work.

- A speech and language pathologist, who specializes in treating communication problems.

- A social worker, who can help patients and their families find financial, educational, and medical assistance in their local communities.

- A psychologist, who helps patients and their families cope with the anxieties, pressures, and demands of cerebral palsy. Sometimes psychologists provide therapy to change unhelpful or destructive behaviors and habits.

- ♦ An educator, who plays an important role when mental impairment or a learning disability presents a challenge to education.

Working Together

Individuals who have cerebral palsy, as well as their families or caregivers, are also important members of the treatment team. They should all be directly involved in all steps of planning, making decisions, and performing the treatments. Studies have shown that family support and personal determination are two of the most important aspects that decide which individuals with cerebral palsy will most likely achieve their long-term goals.

But what if negative issues come into play? Although they may mean well, parents or other family members or caregivers are not always cooperative with the medical, health, and educational professionals who are helping to design the treatment plan. Parents can sometimes interfere too much, or try to control the situation, because they feel they know "what's best" for their child. Or sometimes they do not participate enough, or do not follow through at home with the practicing of therapeutic exercises and skills. They may feel overwhelmed that the care of their child is somehow better left to "the professionals." And what if money is an issue? After all, even with health insurance, isn't the cost of medications, hospitalizations, and the ongoing services of so many medical and health care professionals a worrisome and significant burden?

The partnership between parents and the medical and health care professionals on the treatment team is best when parents have an active but balanced role—demonstrating a real concern for the best interest of their child; taking the advice of knowledgeable specialists and then making informed decisions; and making the skills and exercises that the treatment team provides a part of their child's normal, everyday routine in the home. And, starting with the educational and health care professionals at a child's school, or with the Where to Go for Help section of this book, there are literally dozens of local, state, and federal agencies and nonprofit organizations that can give information about financial assistance and other free support services.

Dealing with Feelings

Okay, you do things differently. You know that your disability interferes with your being able to do all the things that you want. Sometimes people look at and treat you differently than they do others. You feel angry and frustrated.

Perhaps the most important part of living with a disability is dealing with the feelings of anger, frustration, fear, or depression that you may have. But how you see yourself is a big part of how you feel.

Having cerebral palsy does not mean that you cannot excel in and enjoy the same activities as everyone else.

So what can you do to build your self-esteem and change the way that you see yourself?

Plenty. A positive self-image really depends on the support systems you build for yourself, on your being able to come to terms with the medical and emotional issues of your disability, and on your own belief in your value and worth as a human being. Just like anyone else.

Here are some tips on creating a positive self-image for yourself and maintaining good self-esteem:

Communicate

Teens with cerebral palsy face all sorts of obstacles on a daily basis. Seeing doctors and specialists, dealing with their physical differences, and coping with emotional stress may seem completely overwhelming and exhausting at times.

If you are feeling hurt, angry, afraid, or depressed, the most important thing to do is to communicate those feelings. Whether you use words, pictures, sign language, or a communication aid, it really doesn't matter. Just do it. You might keep a journal; you might talk to a friend you trust or a family member; you might see a counselor at school or a therapist your doctor recommends. Expressing your feelings and communicating your fears is the first step in creating a positive self-image of yourself as a person who can both face and overcome obstacles.

Find a support group

Once you have faced the things that are bothering you, you may also find that there are many others out there who share your issues, problems, and questions.

There are numerous agencies, organizations, and Web sites—many of which are listed in the Where to Go for Help section of this book—that can supply you with information on how to find support groups in your area, Internet discussion forums and chat rooms, and 800 hotline numbers. Often, sharing your experiences with others can help you not to feel so alone.

Stay active

Having cerebral palsy does not mean that you cannot enjoy and excel in the same activities and interests as everyone else. So, participate! Get involved in extracurricular activities at your school. Find out what's going on at your local church or temple or mosque. Go out with friends to the movies or museums (public facilities, by law, are wheelchair accessible). Maintain your physical fitness with exercise. Participate in sports, and find out about the Special Olympics if you are competitive!

Create yourself

Remember: Your disability does not define who you are. You define you. So, create yourself! Make yourself the person that you want to be.

Be open and receptive to friendships with others. Make your own decisions—about the clothes you want to wear, the hairstyle you like, the music you listen to, and the foods that you enjoy eating. Make a list of the things that you love to do, and think about why you love doing them so much. And finally, make a list of the things that you would love to do (if you dared), and start working toward making them happen!

When Friends or Family Members Have CP

Often, when we meet someone with cerebral palsy, we don't know how to react to him or her. What do you do if you can't understand what a person is saying? What do you do if you see a person with a disability having trouble in the street? How do you help a person with a disability? Should you, even?

The following are some examples of questions people might have about interacting with someone with CP, and some general rules and hints about disability etiquette—the appropriate way of handling yourself in regard to a person with a disability:

- **How do I talk to someone who has cerebral palsy?** In exactly the same way as you would talk to anyone else the same age. There is no need to yell or speak slowly. And although you may be surprised by the way the person walks or talks, remember, the person is pretty used to his or her disability and is probably hoping that you can see beyond it.

- **What do I do if I can't understand what someone says?** Don't pretend that you can understand when you can't. Let the person know that you didn't understand or hear what was said, and ask the person to repeat what he or she said. Remember, it's always easier to understand what's being said if you look at the person while he or she is talking.

- **How do I talk to someone who can't speak?** Just because a person can't speak, it doesn't mean that he or she can't hear or understand what you're saying. Most people with cerebral palsy can understand normal speech, even if they don't speak themselves.

39

- **What do I do if someone seems to be having trouble walking or managing a wheelchair?** If someone seems to be having difficulty, you might want to offer some assistance. But if the person refuses, then just leave it alone. Never help without asking first! Many people with CP are perfectly happy managing on their own; they just need a little extra time.

- **How do I shake hands with someone with cerebral palsy?** Since people with CP sometimes have trouble controlling their movements, or hold their hands in an unusual way, a simple thing like a handshake can sometimes cause embarrassment or confusion for the person without cerebral palsy. If someone with CP holds out a hand for a handshake, then shake it, exactly the way you would anyone else's hand! However, not everybody wants to shake hands, and people with CP are no exception. The rules for personal contact with someone with a disability are exactly the same as they are with anyone else. Don't feel like you have to stand back, but don't force yourself on someone, either.

- **If I shake hands with someone with cerebral palsy, can I catch it?** Absolutely not! Cerebral palsy is not contagious. It is not a sickness or a disease.

Chapter Four

What Specific Treatments Are Available?

Therapy—whether for movement, speech, or everyday living tasks—is the most important part of treatment for people with cerebral palsy. Some people get therapy at school, and some go to special clinics to see their therapists.

Therapists are professionals who are trained to work with people to help them learn better or easier ways to do things. But no matter what the person's age is, or what kind of therapy is used, treatment does not end when the patient leaves the school, office, or treatment center. In fact, most of the real work is done at home! The therapist is only a part-time coach; the strategies, drills, and skills that are given to parents and patients have to be practiced in order to improve performance at home, at school, and in the world.

There are a number of different kinds of therapies that can be part of a treatment plan for people with cerebral palsy. These include physical therapy, behavioral therapy, speech and language therapy, occupational therapy, and drug therapy.

Physical Therapy

Physical therapy (PT) uses specific exercises to achieve two important goals: preventing a weakening of large muscles (such as those in the arms and legs) that often follows a lack of use, and avoiding "contracture" (when muscles become stiff and fixed in odd positions).

Physical therapists help people learn better ways to move and balance themselves. They may help people with CP learn to walk, use a wheelchair, stand by themselves, or go up and down stairs. Children can work on fun skills like running, throwing a ball, or riding a bike.

Behavioral Therapy

Behavioral therapy uses psychological theory and techniques to increase a person's abilities. For example, behavioral therapy might include hiding a cool prize inside a box to reward a child for learning to reach into it with his or her weaker hand.

Speech and Language Therapy

Speech therapists work with people on communication skills. Communication skills can include talking, using sign language, or using a communication aid (a tool, device, or piece of equipment that helps the person communicate). Children or adults with CP who are able to talk can work with a speech therapist to make their speech clearer and easier to understand, or on building their language skills by learning new words, learning to speak in sentences, or improving their listening skills.

Occupational Therapy

Occupational therapists usually work with children and adults with CP to find better ways to use the smaller muscles in their bodies, like those in the face, hands, feet, fingers, and toes. They may teach children better or easier ways to write, draw, cut with scissors, brush their teeth, dress and feed themselves, or control their wheelchairs.

Drug Therapy

Physicians may prescribe drugs for those who have seizures associated with their cerebral palsy, and these medications are often very effective. In general, the drugs given to individual patients are chosen based on the type of seizures they have, since no one drug controls all types. Drugs are also sometimes used to control spasticity—stiffness or tightness of the muscles—particularly following any kind of surgery.

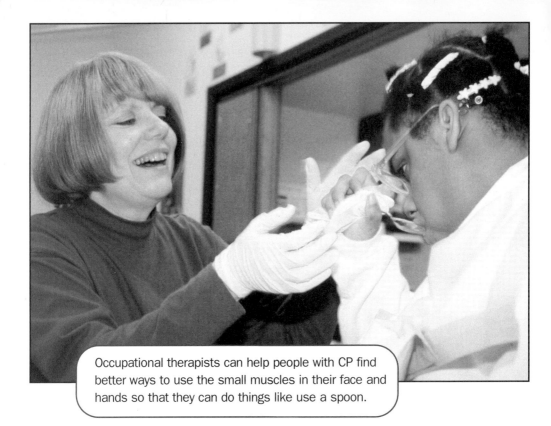

Occupational therapists can help people with CP find better ways to use the small muscles in their face and hands so that they can do things like use a spoon.

Other Treatments

Besides the different forms of therapies, other treatments for cerebral palsy are sometimes employed. These may include surgery and the use of mechanical aids.

Surgery

Sometimes, when muscles are so tight or contracted that they cause severe movement problems, physicians recommend surgery to correct the problem. What a surgeon does is lengthen the muscles and tendons that are too short and tight in order to try and correct the movement problems.

Mechanical aids

Mechanical aids are special tools, devices, or equipment

that people with cerebral palsy might use to help them get around and overcome their particular limitations. These mechanical aids might be anything from a special fork to sophisticated computerized communication devices. Some examples of mechanical aids:

- Adapted silverware and pencils. These are made with special handles or grips, and can be very helpful for someone who has difficulty holding on to small things.

- Communication aids. When a person with CP has speech difficulties, it may be easier for him or her to use a communication aid to talk with others. A communication aid might be a book or a poster that has pictures that show things the person might want, or it might be an alphabet board that can be used to spell out a message.

- Wheelchairs. Wheelchairs allow people with CP who cannot walk, or who have a lot of trouble walking, the ability to move from place to place. Many people with CP can use their arms just fine to roll the wheels of their wheelchairs themselves. Other types of wheelchairs have motors that push the wheels around. A motorized wheelchair has a handle or joystick on it that lets the person using it stop, start, and steer the chair.

When a person with CP has speech difficulties, it may be easier for him or her to use a communication aid to talk with others.

◆ Computers. There are so many things that are available today that can assist people with speech and movement problems to use computers to communicate! There are touch screens, special mouses, and even pointers that fit around the forehead for people who can't use a regular mouse to control the operation of a computer. There are special keyboards with extra large keys, and there are keyboards and special software programs that are created for a person who uses only one hand, or one finger. There are software programs that help people with little or no control of their movement to dial and speak on the phone, or to type only the first couple of letters of a word and then have the computer "predict" what the rest of the word will be! There are also communication aids that can talk for a person by "reading" aloud whatever the person types into the computer.

Sinead, age fifteen, says:

Having CP has given me some really odd and amazing talents. I don't have much movement in my arms or legs, but I can do amazing things with my head! People stand and watch me, and their mouths hang open! I kind of like that. It bugs them out!

I use a power wheelchair and I drive it with my head. The switches to control it are behind me, in the seat. All I have to do to go straight is push my head back; and if I want to go right or left, I turn my head right or left. And there's a switch that I hit with the back of my head to go in reverse.

For my computer, I have a special touch screen and a headband that I wear that has a rod sticking out of it. I'm like a typing unicorn! I move my head forward to touch the screen with the rod and WHAM—I can work a Windows menu and all the commands, or a dozen other special software programs. I can also lean my head down over the keyboard and tap away at the keys. It's a different perspective, but it gets the job done!

Chapter Five

Looking to the Future

There is nothing at present that can cure cerebral palsy or that can prevent it from ever happening to someone. Despite the very best nurturing and medical efforts of parents and doctors, children will still be born today with cerebral palsy. Unfortunately, since in most cases of CP the cause is unknown, little can currently be done to stop it from occurring.

So What Can Be Done?

Thankfully, over the years, there has been research that has identified a few of the causes of cerebral palsy. These particular causes have been shown to be preventable or treatable:

- ◆ Jaundice. Jaundice (as discussed in chapter one) in newborn infants can be treated before it becomes severe enough to cause cerebral palsy. A special procedure called phototherapy is used to treat it. Phototherapy uses special blue lights that break down the yellow bile pigments in an infant's blood before they build up and damage the brain cells.

◆ Rh incompatibility. Rh incompatibility (as discussed in chapter one) is a blood condition where the mother's body produces immune cells called antibodies that can destroy the fetus's blood cells. Today, Rh incompatibility is easily identified by a simple blood test on the pregnant mother. In most cases, a special serum can prevent the unwanted production of antibodies.

◆ Rubella, or German measles. Rubella (as discussed in chapter one) is a virus that can infect pregnant women. This can be prevented if women are vaccinated against the disease before becoming pregnant.

◆ Head injuries. Many head injuries that cause cerebral palsy can be prevented by such things as the regular use of child safety seats while riding in a car; the use of helmets while riding a bicycle, rollerskating, or skateboarding; and eliminating situations of child abuse.

New Research and Therapies

Many scientists and researchers are currently performing studies of the brain and low birthweight, as they explore the causes, treatments, and possible methods of prevention for cerebral palsy.

Exploring the brain

Many scientists believe that if something goes wrong during the early stages of brain development—perhaps the developing brain cells of a fetus don't form in the right way, or they move to wrong areas in the brain, or they don't make the proper connections with the other brain cells—it may cause CP; and they are looking for ways to prevent this from happening before and after birth.

Other areas of research that scientists are exploring are how to prevent seizures, bleeding in the brain, and breathing and circulation problems that threaten the brains of newborn babies.

Exploring low birthweight

Low birthweight is also a subject of much current research in cerebral palsy. Currently, about 7.5 percent of babies born in the United States are low-birthweight or premature babies. Since low-birthweight (5.5 pounds or less) and premature babies are at a higher risk for developing cerebral palsy than full-term (37 weeks developed), normal-weight babies, much scientific attention is being given to exploring new drugs that can delay labor so a baby can be carried full-term, new devices and technology to improve the medical care for low-birthweight and premature infants, and new information about how smoking, alcohol use, and drug abuse can affect the development of an unborn baby.

These two exciting research areas—studies of the brain and studies of low birthweight—offer hope for preventing cerebral palsy in the future.

And as for Now?

As for those who face the challenges of cerebral palsy today, the best hope lies in improving the numerous treatments and therapies that already exist. For example, there is currently research being conducted to identify the exact brain areas controlling specific kinds of movement. By locating brain areas that control specific actions, such as blinking an eye, lifting a leg, or raising an arm, scientists can then make maps of those brain areas. Once they have the maps, they can compare charts made before and after different kinds of therapies to find out how effective a particular kind of therapy is and how it affects the way the brain works.

There is also a great deal of research being done in the development of new drugs, and new ways to use drugs that are already out there, to help relieve such symptoms of cerebral palsy as spasticity, seizures, and epilepsy.

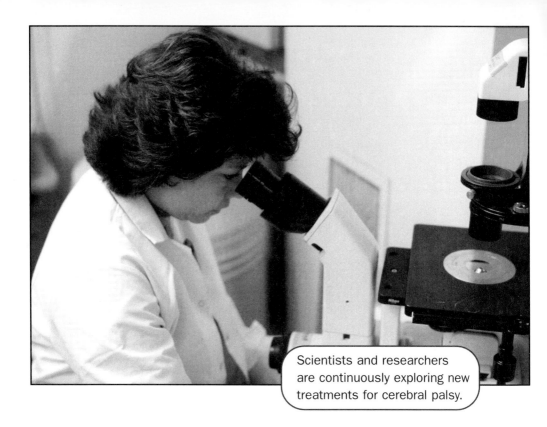

Scientists and researchers are continuously exploring new treatments for cerebral palsy.

As scientists and researchers continue to explore new treatments for cerebral palsy and to increase what we know about how the brain develops in all its early stages, there is good reason to hope and to expect important medical discoveries in the future that will prevent cerebral palsy and many other disorders that happen in early life.

Glossary

acquired cerebral palsy When a person becomes affected by cerebral palsy after birth.

antibodies Immune cells, produced by the body, which fight infections.

ataxic Least common form of cerebral palsy where muscle tone is too low or too loose.

athetoid Form of cerebral palsy where muscle tone is mixed—sometimes too high and sometimes too low.

breech delivery When a baby is delivered buttocks or feet first, instead of head first.

cerebral palsy The overall name given to a group of disorders, caused by an injury to the brain, that affects the way the muscles in the body move.

communication aid A tool used by a person with cerebral palsy who has speech difficulties to talk with others.

computerized tomography (CT) A specialized test that uses X rays and a computer to create a picture of the inside of the brain.

congenital cerebral palsy When the disorder or

disorders associated with cerebral palsy are present at birth.

contracture When muscles become stiff and fixed in odd positions.

developmental delay When a child is slow to reach specific skills and behaviors that are considered normal to have at certain ages.

diplegia When cerebral palsy affects either both arms or both legs.

dysarthria A speech problem associated with cerebral palsy.

electroencephalogram (EEG) A specialized test that records brain activity, given when a doctor suspects a seizure disorder.

epilepsy The condition of having seizures happen over and over without there being a specific reason, such as a high fever.

failure to thrive A general term doctors use to describe children who seem to fall behind in growth and development.

fetus A developing baby still in the mother's womb.

hemiplegia When cerebral palsy affects only one side of the body, such as just the right arm and leg or just the left arm and leg.

jaundice A condition that can damage brain tissue, caused by a build-up of bile pigments in the blood.

learning disability Difficulty processing certain kinds of information in a person with normal intelligence; a form of mental impairment associated with cerebral palsy.

Little's disease   The disorder, which is now known as spastic diplegia, named for the English surgeon William Little who first wrote about it.

low birthweight   Weighing 5.5 pounds or less at birth.

magnetic resonance imaging (MRI)   A specialized test that creates an image of the brain using magnetic fields and radio waves.

monoplegia   When cerebral palsy affects only one limb.

Moro reflex   An automatic gesture or reflex that a baby makes with its arms (and which looks like a hug) when a doctor places it on its back with the legs raised above the head.

motor areas   Those parts of the brain that control movement and posture.

obstetrician   A doctor who delivers babies.

occupational therapist   A therapist who helps individuals improve the development of their small muscle movement (face, hands, feet, fingers, toes).

ophthalmologist   An eye doctor.

orthopedist   A doctor who specializes in treating the bones, muscles, tendons, and other parts of the body's skeletal system.

otologist   An ear doctor.

pediatrician   A doctor who treats children.

pediatric neurologist   A doctor who specializes in brain disorders in children.

phototherapy   A treatment for jaundice that uses special blue lights to break down bile pigments in the blood before they build up and damage brain cells.

physical therapist (PT) A therapist who creates special exercise programs to improve a patient's movement and strength in the large muscles of the body (arms, legs, torso).

premature Babies born early (before 37 weeks' time).

quadriplegia When cerebral palsy affects all limbs on both sides of the body.

Rh incompatibility A blood condition where the mother's body produces immune cells (antibodies) that destroy the fetus's blood cells.

rubella Another name for German measles, which is caused by a virus that can infect pregnant women.

seizure A sudden attack brought on by a series of abnormal electrical messages in the brain being sent out very close together.

spastic When muscles in the body are very tight and stiff.

strabismus A disorder, associated with cerebral palsy, where the eyes do not line up and focus properly because of differences between the left and right eye muscles.

stroke An injury to the brain caused by internal bleeding.

triplegia When cerebral palsy affects three limbs.

ultrasonography A specialized test that creates an image of the brain using sound waves.

viral encephalitis A severe brain infection that can cause acquired cerebral palsy.

Where to Go for Help

Organizations

Epilepsy Foundation of America
4351 Garden City Drive
Landover, MD 20785
(301) 577-4941
(800) 332-1000
http://www.efa.org

Learning Disabilities Association of America
4156 Library Road
Pittsburgh, PA 15234
(412) 341-1515
http://www.ldanatl.org

March of Dimes Birth Defects Foundation
1275 Mamaroneck Avenue
White Plains, NY 10605
(914) 428-7100
http://www.modimes.org

National Easter Seal Society
230 West Monroe Street, Suite 1800
Chicago, IL 60606
(312) 726-6200
(800) 221-6827
http://www.seals.com

National Institute of Neurological Disorders
  and Stroke (NINDS)
National Institutes of Health
31 Center Drive MSC 2540
Bethesda, MD 20892
(301) 496-5751
(800) 352-9424
http://www.ninds.nih.gov

National Rehabilitation Information Center (NARIC)
1010 Wayne Avenue, Suite 800
Silver Spring, MD 20910-5633
(301) 562-2400
(800) 346-2742
http://www.naric.com/naric

United Cerebral Palsy Associations
1660 L Street N.W., Suite 700
Washington, DC 20036
(202) 776-0406
(800) 872-5827
http://www.ucpa.org

800 Numbers
Americans with Disabilities Act (ADA)
(800) 949-4232

National Head Injury Foundation
(800) 444-6443

National Information Center for
Children and Youth with Disabilities
(800) 695-0285

Information Web Sites
Kid's PT—Cerebral Palsy
http://www.geocities.com/hotsprings/spa/5965/cp.htm

Cerebral Palsy Info Central
http://members.aol.com/anee/index.html

Cerebral Palsy: A Multimedia Tutorial for Children and
    Parents
http://www.med.virginia.edu/cmc/tutorials/cp/

Cerebral Palsy Support Network
http://www.home.aone.net.au/cpsn

Cerebral Palsy—Center for Current Research
http://wellweb.com/INDEX/QCEREBRA.HTM

Healthtouch—Cerebral Palsy
http://www.healthtouch.com/level1/leaflets/113966/113966.
htm

Other CP Friends' Web Sites
Adam's Page and Virtual Gallery
http://www.geocities.com/SoHo/Gallery/7161

Carla's Place
http://www.brunnet.net/terrier

The Craig Family Homepage
http://www.cyberscrapbook.com

Dona's CP Email Penpal Page
http://www.proaxis.com/~donad

Kid Power
http://www.geocities.com/Heartland/Village/
    9021/index.html

Narelle's Page
http://www.geocities.com/Heartland/Ridge/9773

The Ramp Ahead
http://wkweb4.cableinet.co.uk/robert.softley

Susie's Cerebral Palsy Homepage
http://www.susiecphome.com/home.html

On-line CP Discussion Forums
UCP Discussion Groups
http://www.ucpa.org/html/discussion/index.html

Tell Us Your Story
http://www.tell-us-your-story.com

On-line CP Newsgroup
alt.support.cerebral-palsy

On-line CP Chat Room

CPN's Chat Pad
http://www.geocities.com/Heartland/Plains/
    8950/enter.html

For Further Reading

Books

Brown, Christy. *My Left Foot*. London: Mandarin Books, 1989.

Geralis, Elaine, ed. *Children with Cerebral Palsy: A Parent's Guide*. Bethesda, MD: Woodbine House, 1998.

Leonard, Jane Faulkner, and Sherri L. Cadenhead. *Keys to Parenting a Child with Cerebral Palsy*. Hauppauge, NY: Barron's Educational Series, 1997.

Little, Jean. *Mine for Keeps*. Ontario, Canada: Viking Press, 1994.

Martin, Ann M. *Karen's New Friend*. New York: Scholastic, 1993.

Metzger, Lois. *Barry's Sister*. New York: Atheneum Press, 1993.

Metzger, Lois. *Ellen's Case*. New York: Atheneum Press, 1995.

Mikaelson, Ben. *Petey*. New York: Hyperion Press, 1998.

Smith, Mark. *Growing Up with Cerebral Palsy*. Waco, TX: WRS Publishing, 1995.

On-line Books

The entire book *Moon Gate Dreams: My Life with Cerebral Palsy*, by George A. Barker Jr., can be read on-line by going to *http:www.mycerebralpalsy.com* .

Films

A Day at a Time. Dir. William Garcia. New York: Filmaker's Library, 1992.

My Left Foot. Dir. Jim Sheridan. With Daniel Day-Lewis, Ray McAnally, and Brenda Fricker. Miramax, 1989.

Index

Index

About the Author

Dion Pincus is a writer and a teacher, and has worked with individuals with disabilities for the past fifteen years. He has designed service delivery models and run programs for students with disabilities at numerous City University of New York colleges, and was the founder and executive director of the AccessAbility Project, a nonprofit educational organization providing academic and vocational support services for youth and adults with disabilities.

Photo Credits

Cover by Thaddeus Harden. P. 2 © United Cerebral Palsy; p. 10 © Jeff Greenberg/Photo Researchers, Inc.; p. 18 © ATC Production/Custom Medical Stock Photo; p. 23 © Blair Seitz/Photo Researchers, Inc.; pp. 33, 44 © Jeff Greenberg/The Image Works; p. 36 © Carl J. Single/The Image Works; p. 46 © B. Daemmrich/The Image Works; p. 52 by Seth Dinnerman.